This Book Belongs to...

....

LONDON, NEW YORK, MELBOURNE, MUNICH, AND DELHI

Editor Charlie Gardner
Designer Wendy Bartlet
Production Editor Melissa Latorre
Production Controller Jen Lockwood
U.S. Editor Jennifer Quasha

First published in the United States in 2009
by DK Publishing
375 Hudson Street
New York, New York 10014

09 10 11 12 13 10 9 8 7 6 5 4 3 2
SD425—07/09

DK books are available at special discounts when purchased in bulk for
sales promotions, premiums, fundraising, or educational use. For details, contact:
DK Publishing Special markets
375 Hudson Street
New York, New York 10014
specialSales@dk.com

A catalog record for this book is
available from the Library of Congress.

ISBN: 978-0-7566-5230-2

Printed and bound in China by L-Rex

Discover more at
www.dk.com

The publisher would like to thank the following for
their kind permission to reproduce their photographs:

(Key: a-above; b-below/bottom; c-center; f-far; l-left; r-right; t-top)

Alamy Images: Duncan Shaw 5b, 20cr. Alvey and Towers: 10-11, (sticker sheet) 11tr, 19tl, 20cl (sticker sheet).
Corbis: Richard Cummins 17cra; Kimberly White 7b.
DK Images: Cockermouth Mountain Rescue Team, England 12, (sticker sheet) 13br, 13tr, 19tr, 20tr;
RAF Boulmer, Northumberland 1tl, 17tr, 20tl (sticker sheet); Volunteer Medical Service Corps, Lansdale, PA 6-7,
7tr, (sticker sheet) 14-15 (sticker sheet) 15t, 18cl, 19cl, 20bl. Getty Images: Check Six 17b; National Geographic / Raul Touzon 5tr.
iStockphoto.com: Daniel Cardiff 16-17, 19br (sticker sheet); Matt Richard 15br (sticker sheet);
Christophe Testi 3, 4, 18tr (sticker sheet); Terry Wilson 9br. Jacket images: DK Images: VMS Corps, Lansdale, PA.

All other images © Dorling Kindersley
For further information see: www.dkimages.com

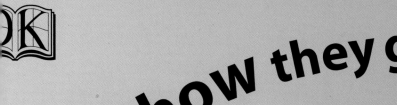

See how they go

Emergency vehicles

Fantastic fire truck

CA

SIREN

I AM A FIRE TRUCK

SEE HOW I GO!

DANGER
ELECTROCUTION HAZARD
KEEP CLEAR

Look at me. I am a great big water tank on wheels. My powerful pumps can squirt jets of water up at tall buildings.

I have lockers full of tools and rescue equipment, too.

HOSE

FIRE EXTINGUISHER

When I get to an emergency, my firefighters connect my hoses and get to work.

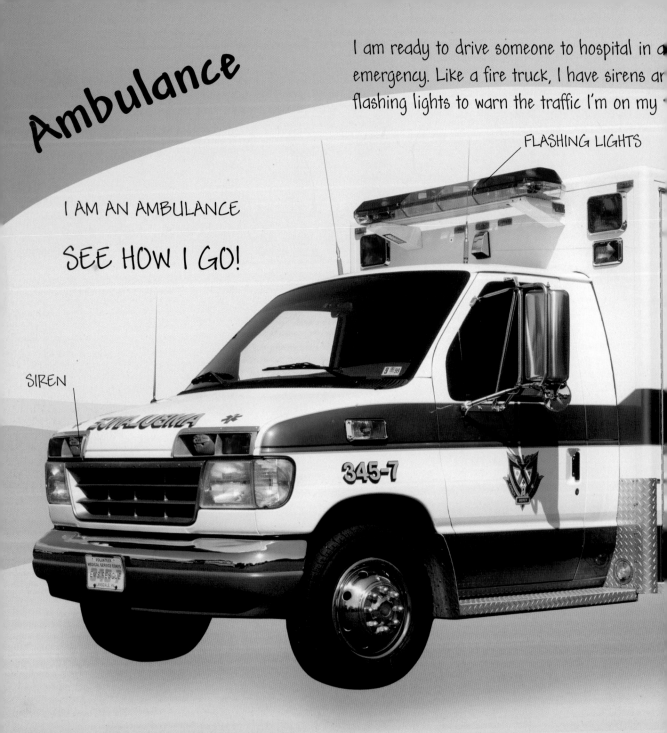

Ambulance

I am ready to drive someone to hospital in a
emergency. Like a fire truck, I have sirens an
flashing lights to warn the traffic I'm on my

FLASHING LIGHTS

I AM AN AMBULANCE

SEE HOW I GO!

SIREN

345-7

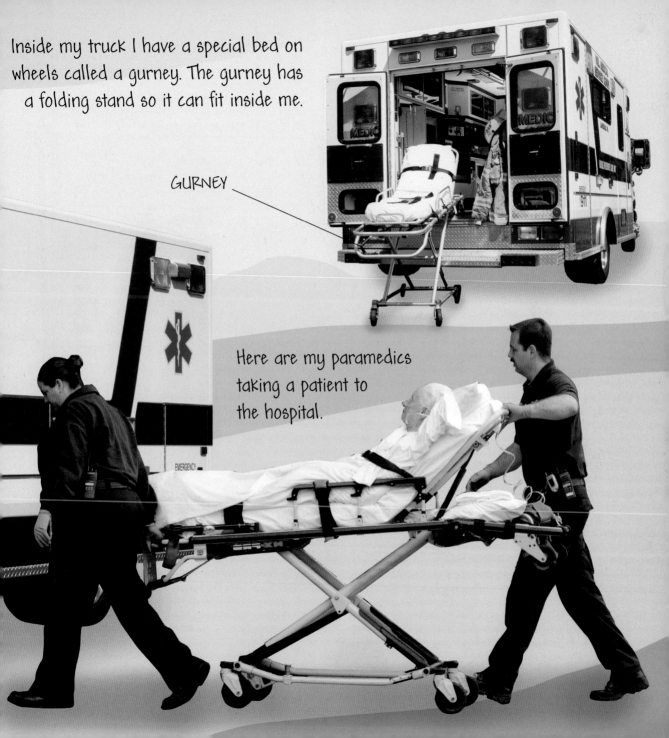

Inside my truck I have a special bed on wheels called a gurney. The gurney has a folding stand so it can fit inside me.

GURNEY

Here are my paramedics taking a patient to the hospital.

Terrific tow truck

I tow vehicles that have broken down.

EXHAUST
PIPE

HORN

I AM A TOW TRUCK

SEE HOW I GO!

40

3810·HV

FUEL
TANK

BOOM

SLING

Have you ever seen a tow truck as big as me before? I am a heavy-duty tow truck, built to rescue trucks and buses.

Look at me lifting my smaller friend!

Sometimes my driver can fix a vehicle on the road. If not, I will tow it to a garage.

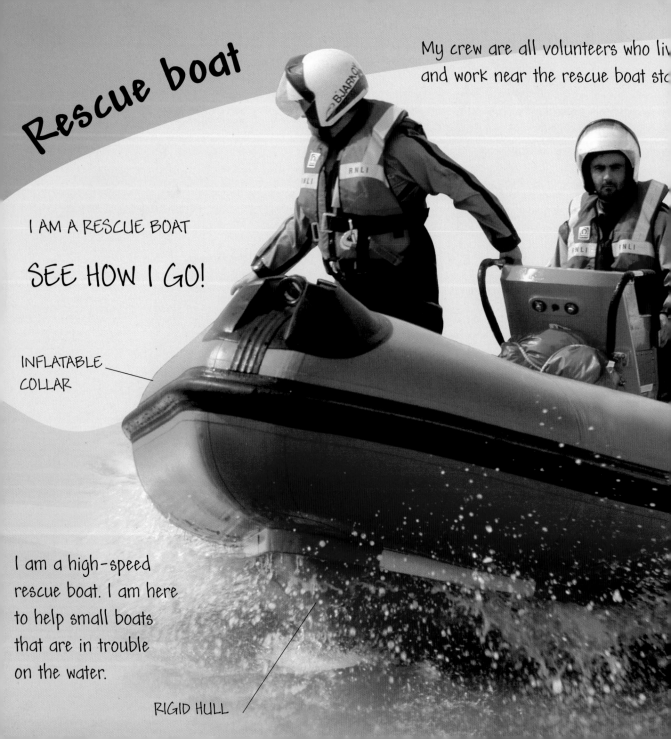

Rescue boat

My crew are all volunteers who liv and work near the rescue boat sto

I AM A RESCUE BOAT

SEE HOW I GO!

INFLATABLE
COLLAR

I am a high-speed
rescue boat. I am here
to help small boats
that are in trouble
on the water.

RIGID HULL

RADIO ANTENNA

OUTBOARD
MOTOR

Here's my friend, a jet-ski rescue boat. He is just the right size to rescue swimmers and surfers who need help near the shore.

I am a rigid inflatable boat, or RIB for short. I have a light, strong, stiff plastic hull and a huge inflatable collar around my sides. This cushion of air keeps me afloat in stormy seas.

Marvelous mountaineer

I AM A MOUNTAIN RESCUE TRUCK

SEE HOW I GO!

If a mountain climber is in danger, I take a rescue team close by.

FLASHING LIGHTS

WINCH

I can drive off road and up steep hills. I carry eight rescuers, all of them mountaineers.

I have special equipment
like stretchers, lights,
sleeping bags, ropes,
axes, and maps.

ROPES

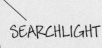

SEARCHLIGHT

MUD
FLAP

My rescue team unload
just what they need, then
set out on foot to help.

Snowmobile

I AM A SNOW RESCUE VEHICLE

SEE HOW I GO!

I am a snowmobile ambulance that rescues people in snow. Ambulances on wheels can't go where I go.

SKI

I am a motorized sled. I have caterpillar tracks to grip the ice, and skis on the front.

My paramedic rides me like a motorcycle, and turns my handlebars to steer me.

HANDLEBARS

Behind me, I tow a covered trailer. It's just big enough for a stretcher.

STRETCHER

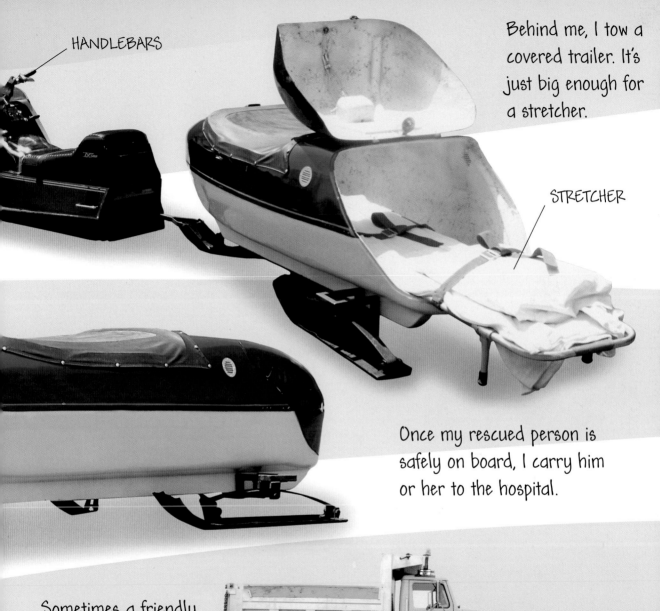

Once my rescued person is safely on board, I carry him or her to the hospital.

Sometimes a friendly snowplow helps clear my route.

Helicopter helper

Here I am hovering over a boat, ready to rescue a sailor who has broken his leg.

I AM A RESCUE HELICOPTER

SEE HOW I GO!

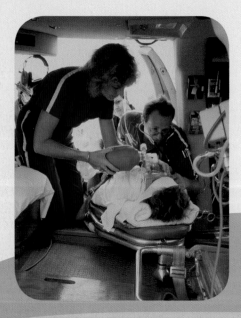

LANDING GEAR

WINCH OPERATOR

I am specially designed to help people in trouble at sea or in other remote areas.

OTOR
LADE

TAIL
ROTOR

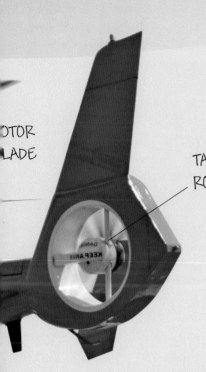

Now we are off to the hospital. This hospital has a helipad so I can land on its roof.

a long steel cable
to lower my winch
erator down to the
t. Then he attaches
sailor to the winch
I lift both of them
back inside.

See how they go!

FIRE TRUCK

AMBULANCE

TOW TRUCK

MOUNTAIN RESCUE VEHICLE

RESCUE BOAT

OWMOBILE AMBULANCE

RESCUE HELICOPTER

See How They GO!

Other titles:

Fire Truck

ISBN 978-0-7566-4553-3

Train

ISBN 978-0-7566-4552-6

Trucks

ISBN 978-0-7566-5168-8

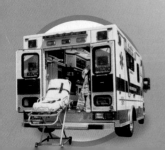

Diggers

ISBN 978-0-7566-5167-1

Cars

ISBN 978-07566-5231-9